A THRILL OF hope

House
on a
Hill Co.

A THRILL OF *hope*

A Thrill of Hope
Published by House on a Hill Co.
419 E. 8th St. Ashland, OH 44805 U.S.A

Unless otherwise noted, all Scripture quotations are taken from the Holy Bible, English Standard Version, ESV.

ISBN 979-8-343-544-107

First Edition

Endorsements

At a time of year that feels busy and rushed and often leaves us weary, Chelsey reminds us of the hope we have in Jesus—not just this time of year but always. A Thrill of Hope is an invitation to slow down as we prepare our hearts to celebrate the birth of Christ. You will love this devotional if you desire a more hope-filled advent season.
-Sarah Nichols, Content Writer for Intentional Living and iBelieve

A Thrill of Hope is a beautiful reminder of what we all need to focus on this Christmas season—Jesus. Chelsey shares the hope of Jesus in a relatable, encouraging way and shows us what it looks like to focus on His light even when our world feels dark. This truly is the perfect devotional for your Christmas season!
-Mandy Johnson, writer, speaker, and Online Community Host for Esther Press Women Publishing

This Advent devotional is a brilliant mix of God's Word, the words of Oh Holy Night, and Chelsey's own words. The three blend beautifully to offer an intimate reflection of God's Glory in light of the Thrill of Hope we experience through a personal relationship with Jesus Christ. Chelsey's intimacy with the Savior is evident in her words, and I trust God will use this devotional to draw you closer to Him as well.
-Tabitha Deller, author of Called, Brave, Near, and Stay

We all want to soak in deeply the divine awe, wonder, and hope offered in the celebration season of Jesus's birth. And I found the precious pages of this devotion, A Thrill of Hope, to be the perfect daily preparation to connect my heart to His. What a wonderful way to recenter our souls with our Savior, to unleash the glorious light of world, and then shine his love and hope even brighter as we magnify our Messiah!
-Keri Eichberger, Author of Win over Worry

Dedication

A Thrill of Hope is dedicated to Bob Thiel, my Grampa, who went to be with Jesus on June 6, 2024. His life marked mine in the most beautiful way. His hunger to know Jesus and understand a life walking with God even till the end leaves me changed forever.

He is now living in the presence of Jesus. He is experiencing eternal hope. Rejoicing with a heart full of peace. Resting in God's immense, unending, and unchanging love.

Grampa, I miss you more than words can express, thank you for always voicing how proud you were of me. It was the honor of a lifetime to be your only granddaughter. I can't wait to be with you again soon. And this next time, we'll be in eternity together - **forever**. To God be the glory!

But, as it is written,
"What no eye has seen, nor ear heard,
nor the heart of man imagined, what God has
prepared for those who love him.."
1 Corinthians 2:9

A message from Chelsey

The prayer behind A Thrill of Hope is for you to spend the Advent season reflecting on the gift we received when Jesus was born. Without Jesus' birth, true everlasting peace wouldn't be possible and our hope wouldn't be secure. The life of our Savior in the flesh made a way for us to live with the hope of all that is to come while journeying through the joys and trenches of our life on this side of heaven.

In the pages of this devotional you'll find personal stories from my life, scripture teachings, prayer prompts, and journal pages to draw your heart closer to Christ. I pray this advent season will be one where you seek the hope we have because of Christ's coming and understand what a gift it is to be in a relationship with Him.

All scripture references are from the ESV translation.

Table of Contents

O' Holy Night

She will bear a son, and you shall call his name Jesus, for he will save his people from their sins. Luke 1:21

The season we most often anticipate is among us. Advent is here and the reminder of our hope being secured sears in our hearts all over again. This Christmas season will mark the first time celebrating without one of my most treasured family members. Perhaps you, too, have experienced all the feelings that come with the loss of someone dear to you during a time where the rest of the world seems to be joyful. It's new, it's different, but my hope is not lost.

As I settled in my cozy brown chair and began writing, the grief once again washed over me. However, for the first time in almost a year, the grief was met almost instantly with the reminder of the joy I can have within my circumstances because of Jesus. He is the gift of light in the darkness. He is the gift of peace in the waves of the storms. We see this by the way Jesus came as a precious baby. His arrival, though it seemed lowly, pierced the darkness forever.

He brought forth the light of the world and the gospel of peace to a world that was wearily waiting for their Savior.

The night Christ was born was deemed holy and perfect. The night of His birth delivered the invitation humanity had been waiting for. The gift of a Savior, the redeemer, the ultimate counselor, the perfect friend, the sustainer through all of life, and the giver of the eternal light that will never be dimmed.

As you settle into this season, whether filled with joy or finding yourself in waves of grief, cling to the reminder that hope has come. Jesus is with you and will meet your every need, seek Him in the stillness.

Prayer Prompt

Father, thank you for sending your perfect Son. He is the greatest gift and the reason I am able to be filled with hope during the hard days. Steady me this season. In Jesus' name, amen.

Takeaway

_____

_____

_____

_____

_____

_____

_____

_____

_____

_____

_____

_____

_____

_____

She will bear a son, and you shall call his name Jesus, for he will save his people from their sins.

Luke 1:21

Brightly Shining

No one could see anyone else or move about for three days. Yet all the Israelites had light in the places where they lived. Exodus 10:23

One of my favorite stories in the whole Bible is when God sends the plague of darkness over all of Egypt when Pharaoh refused to let the Israelites go. In Exodus 10, darkness fell and covered Egypt for three days and we read in verse 23, "No one could see anyone else or move about for three days. Yet all the Israelites had light in the places where they lived."

All of God's people had light where they lived. It doesn't say some people had light on one day or that the light was only for a few moments, the light shone around all of His people for three days as the rest of Egypt sat in darkness.

This light spoken of in Exodus is the same light that Jesus brought to the world when He came, when He died, and when He defeated the grave. We are given this same light and called to shine it brightly wherever God places us.

In this season that can be filled with such joy but also such pain, what if we used this time of celebrating the birth of Jesus by shining brightly for Him? Think of all that could happen if we took these next few weeks to shine the light of Christ in our homes and communities.

The light we carry scatters the darkness. It removes fear and hopelessness. The light of Jesus sends the enemy and his tactics back to their rightful place - away from the hearts and minds of believers. Jesus came to bring His light and spread His love, then called His people to shine His light brightly to all the world.

Prayer Prompt

Father, thank you for sending your Son to bring the light that resides in all believers. Help me shine brightly for you in all the places you send me. Make me bold and brave for you and your Kingdom. In Jesus' name, amen.

Takeaway

_____

_____

_____

_____

_____

_____

_____

_____

_____

_____

_____

_____

_____

No one could see anyone else or move about for three days. Yet all the Israelites had light in the places where they lived.

Exodus 10:23

Soul Felt It's Worth

And behold, you will conceive in your womb and bear a son, and you shall call his name Jesus. Luke 1:31

The season of advent often leaves me reflecting on the first Christmas season I spent walking with Jesus. I was hopeful and expectant. I was filled with joy knowing that I knew the One I was celebrating. My soul finally felt it's worth.

I was overcome by emotion at the truth that God sent His own son, who would be perfect, holy, and blameless to be the One that would bridge the gap for eternity with me. This was a worth I had never known before. A worth wrapped in love, forgiveness, correction, and care. It melted my heart of stone and left me changed forever.

It reminds me of the way Mary must've felt when she received the news that she would be the one to bring forth God's son into the world. I'm sure she felt a worth that she had never experienced - and it changed her life forever.

"And the angel said to her, "Do not be afraid, Mary, for you have found favor with God. And behold, you will conceive in your womb and bear a son, and you shall call his name Jesus." Luke 1:30-31

The love of God and the pursuit of God is so powerful. His love and pursuit change the way we see ourselves and gives us a clear view of how much He loves us. God didn't send His son to this world because He liked us. He sent His son because He loves us so much that He didn't want to be eternally separated from us.

God showed us how worth it we are to Him. He made a way to live life with us - forever. What a God we serve!

Prayer Prompt

Father, thank you for the gift of eternal life. I am deeply grateful you chose to pursue me and save me through the sending of your son, Jesus. Help me to never take this gift for granted. In Jesus' name, amen.

Takeaway

And behold, you will conceive in your womb and bear a son, and you shall call his name Jesus.

Luke 1:21

The Weary World Rejoices

For to us a child is born, to us a son is given, and the government will be on his shoulders. And he will be called Wonderful Counselor, Mighty God, Everlasting Father, Prince of Peace. Isaiah 9:6

"Rejoice! Rejoice! Emmanuel. Shall come to thee, O Israel." What beautiful lyrics given to us through a song that paints the picture of immense joy within the hearts of those who had long awaited the Messiah's coming. It's interesting to me that though there was an entire nation waiting for Christ's coming, some chose not to believe when the prophecy was fulfilled. Why, some of us ask? Because the way Jesus came was too lowly and not fit for a king.

How often do we miss seeing Jesus because we're thinking the same way many Jewish people thought over 2000 years ago? We somehow find ourselves believing the lie that the King of Kings couldn't possibly want to reveal Himself in a seemingly lowly way. I've certainly found myself thinking like this, passing off ordinary moments as if they are nothing, when really, they are something special to God.

As I've walked with Jesus, I've found that I see Him most often in the places you and I wouldn't expect to find a King. He meets me in the valleys, He meets me in the dark hours of the night, He meets me when my worries and fears begin to swirl. He draws me in and reveals Himself to me all over again.

Something shifts when we go looking for Jesus. It changes the way we live and the way we love. It softens the hardness of our hearts and reveals the depth of God's love for us.

Jesus dwelled among us and now dwells within us. His coming set us free and offered us the gift of eternity with Him. Because of that, we shall rejoice!

Prayer Prompt

Father, thank you for sending your Son to dwell among us and to show us that He meets us in the lowly. I pray that my heart seeks to see you in the valleys of life and in the mountain top moments. You are a faithful Father. In Jesus' name, amen.

Takeaway

_____

_____

_____

_____

_____

_____

_____

_____

_____

_____

_____

_____

_____

For to us a child is born, to us a son is given, and the government will be on his shoulders. And he will be called Wonderful Counselor, Mighty God, Everlasting Father, Prince of Peace.

Isaiah 9:6

A New and Glorious Morn

Go therefore and make disciples of all nations, baptizing them in the name of the Father and of the Son and of the Holy Spirit. Matthew 28:19

Everyone loves a fresh start. It's an invitation for new beginnings, newfound wisdom, and an opportunity to see things from a better perspective. I love this time of year for that very reason. Advent causes me to pause and reflect on how I've seen Jesus all year.

Some years the "heart check" inventory is filled with seeing Jesus in more highs than lows, and some years it's the opposite. Regardless of what the inventory reveals, I always notice the new beginnings I was offered that flow from my relationship with Christ.

Part of Jesus' coming was for the very reason that we would get a new beginning, with Him. A new life where He is the leader and Lord over all we do. A new life where He is our Sustainer and Counselor. A new life where He is King of our hearts.

What a glorious gift. A gift that we must celebrate and treasure. A gift that we must go and tell about... read these words Jesus spoke to His disciples when He gave the great commission. "All authority in heaven and on earth has been given to me. Therefore go and make disciples of all nations, baptizing them in the name of the Father and of the Son and of the Holy Spirit, and teaching them to obey everything I have commanded you. And surely I am with you always, to the very end of the age." Matthew 28:18-20

The Gospel message is the new beginning that we have the ability to teach and share with those God has put in our midst. Jesus, our King who arrived in a manger, has commissioned us to do so and has prepared us fully. Let this be the Advent season where you share the glorious hope we have because of Christ's coming.

Prayer Prompt

Father, thank you for the gift of new beginnings. Your grace and mercy flow forth through our surrender to walk with Jesus. Give me the opportunity to share the gospel message this Advent season. In Jesus' name, amen.

Takeaway

_____

_____

_____

_____

_____

_____

_____

_____

_____

_____

_____

_____

_____

Go therefore and make disciples of all nations, baptizing them in the name of the Father and of the Son and of the Holy Spirit.

Matthew 28:19

Fall on Your Knees

Peace I leave with you; My peace I give to you; not as the world gives do I give to you. Do not let your heart be troubled, nor let it be fearful. John 14:27

There is one specific memory that stands out most of me falling on my knees before Jesus. I was in my tiny studio apartment wanting so desperately to hear what God wanted me to do with my life. I was lonely, tired, and honestly - fearful for what the future held.

To my knees I fell. With tears and a desperate cry for help from my Savior I asked him to show me where I needed to go and what steps I needed to take. I deeply desired for God's plans to be evident before me. Then, Jesus met me. Not with plans, not with a calling, but with His peace.

I learned that night how the presence of God moves us to a posture of peacefulness. He didn't change my circumstance, but He met me in the midst of it. He calmed the fears and breathed new breath into my weary bones. This caused me to go looking for the ways the Spirit of God covered those with peace who had gone before me in the faith.

2 Corinthians 13:11, "Finally, brethren, rejoice, be made complete, be comforted, be like-minded, live in peace; and the God of love and peace will be with you."

Isaiah 26:3, "He whose mind is stayed on you will be in perfect peace, because he trusts in you."

John 14:27, "Peace I leave with you; My peace I give to you; not as the world gives do I give to you. Do not let your heart be troubled, nor let it be fearful."

His peace did not come in the absence of trials for believer's long ago, and the same is true today. His peace is what guided them and guides us through them. If you're feeling weary and wanting the peace of Christ, surrender what it is you're carrying and ask Him for the evidence that He is with you. He will be faithful.

Prayer Prompt

Father, thank you for the peace you've given me because of Jesus. Help me seek you when I'm facing trials. Help me see you when I'm weary. Lead my heart closer to yours. In Jesus' name, amen.

Takeaway

_____

_____

_____

_____

_____

_____

_____

_____

_____

_____

_____

_____

_____

_____

Peace I leave with you; My peace I give to you; not as the world gives do I give to you. Do not let your heart be troubled, nor let it be fearful.

John 14:27

Oh Hear the Angels Voices

And behold, you will conceive in your womb and bear a son, and you shall call his name Jesus. Luke 1:31

Can you imagine what it would've been like to be Mary receiving the news that she would be carrying the Savior of the World in her womb? Exciting, overwhelming, full of awe and wonder. Maybe she felt all of those at once.

"And behold, you will conceive in your womb and bear a son, and you shall call his name Jesus. He will be great and will be called the Son of the Most High. And the Lord God will give to him the throne of his father David, and he will reign over the house of Jacob forever, and of his kingdom there will be no end." Luke 1:31-33

When I imagine Mary hearing the words she had "found favor in sight of God", the Holy Spirit stirs in my heart that I've found favor in His sight too. It just looks different. Sometimes it's exciting, at times feels overwhelming, but mostly leaves me in awe that God wants to use me for His Kingdom.

25

The favor and blessings of God have fallen on and in the hearts of those who love Him. The seal of salvation has been placed on our lives and His purpose for each believer holds Kingdom significance, just like Mary.

It's important to note the way the angel began speaking to Mary, too. "Do not be afraid". This speaks so tenderly to my heart, and I pray the same for your heart, too. As God prompts and prepares us, for Kingdom work, He reminds us to not be afraid. He tells us to remember that we have found favor with Him - the God of all Creation.

As we march forward in our faith with ears attuned to the voice of God, may we seek to trust where He leads us. Let us not be afraid when He speaks but emboldened by the gift it is as He makes His plans clear. Remember - you are a favored child of God.

Prayer Prompt

Father, thank you for speaking to me through your Word. Help me as I lean in and listen for your still small voice. In Jesus' name, amen.

Takeaway

_____

_____

_____

_____

_____

_____

_____

_____

_____

_____

_____

_____

_____

And behold, you will conceive in your womb and bear a son, and you shall call his name Jesus.

Luke 1:31

O' Night Divine

And the Word became flesh and dwelt among us, and we have seen his glory, glory as of the only Son from the Father, full of grace and truth. John 1:14

Have you ever experienced a moment that felt completely divine? As if it were so sacred you'd wish you could've captured it and preserved it forever? Well, when Jesus entered this world in the quiet of the night over 2000 years ago, it was the divine moment that changed the trajectory of life for everyone, forever. Heaven had finally come to dwell on earth. No longer was seeing or experiencing heaven but a glimpse. Heaven was here in the flesh. And while Jesus' earthly ministry didn't feel long enough, it was exactly what was needed to show the goodness of God, the mystery of God, the grace of God.

"And the Word became flesh and dwelt among us, and we have seen his glory, glory as of the only Son from the Father, full of grace and truth. (John bore witness about him, and cried out, "This was he of whom I said, 'He who comes after me ranks before me

because he was before me.'") For from his fullness we have all received, grace upon grace. For the law was given through Moses; grace and truth came through Jesus Christ. No one has ever seen God; the only God, who is at the Father's side, he has made him known.
John 1:14-18

I'm often taken over by emotion at the reality that glory came down to dwell with us. As people who would never be able to repay the debt that we owed, it's a gift I don't think we'll ever fully grasp on this side of heaven. The One who ranks the highest of all, the King of Kings and Lord of Lords came to make us right with God so we could dwell with Him forever.

What a divine. sacred, and irreplaceable gift we've received. Heaven has come and our hope is secured.

Prayer Prompt

Father, thank you for sending your perfect Son. I pray that my life would emulate Christ and my life would be an offering to you. Help me grow closer to you as I seek you in everyday moments. In Jesus' name, amen.

Takeaway

_____

_____

_____

_____

_____

_____

_____

_____

_____

_____

_____

_____

_____

And the Word became flesh and dwelt among us, and we have seen his glory, glory as of the only Son from the Father, full of grace and truth.

John 1:14

Led by the Light of Faith

And an angel of the Lord appeared to them, and the glory of the Lord shone around them, and they were filled with great fear. Luke 2:9

We've all experienced the power going out or not being able to get the light on fast enough to figure out what the sound was we just heard. The light breathes ease into our souls. It reveals safety and brings security. It shows us a way forward and a way out of somewhere we may not want to be.

Growing up I feared the dark; I slept with a nightlight in my room till I went off to college. The darkness brought a feeling I couldn't shake. It made my body tense from head to toe. Then once I became a Christian, it became clear to me why the darkness caused me to feel so unsettled. God created His people to seek the light, live in light of eternity, and experience a life with the Light of the world - His Son, Jesus. My heart didn't crave "light" all those years just because - my heart was craving the Savior to rule it.

Luke 2:9 says, "And an angel of the Lord appeared to them, and the glory of the Lord shone around them, and they were filled with great fear." When the shepherds were out watching their flock, it was the glory of the Lord that pierced the darkness. Their fear fled when they realized this great light was delivering them and giving them the message of good news that would bring great joy to all people who would come to know Christ.

As we flee the darkness and crave the light, may we find our steadiness and hope in Jesus while we make Him known to those around us. Shine brightly where you are, lead boldly by faith, and be led into God's glory.

Prayer Prompt

Father, thank you for creating the desire in me to seek the Light of the world, which is your Son, Jesus. Help me to shine brightly where you have me, make me bold to lead faithfully, and I pray to see your glory on display through my obedience to you. In Jesus' name, amen.

Takeaway

_____

_____

_____

_____

_____

_____

_____

_____

_____

_____

_____

_____

_____

And an angel of the Lord appeared to them, and the glory of the Lord shone around them, and they were filled with great fear.

Luke 2:9

With Glowing Hearts

May the God of hope fill you with all joy and peace in believing, so that by the power of the Holy Spirit you may abound in hope. Romans 15:13

Hope in Christ is what keeps us going. It keeps us walking forward faithfully, even when we feel like we're clinging to Jesus' robe to keep our head above the water. Hope steadies us. It stills the swirling thoughts. It gives way to peace and joy. Hope is ours because of Jesus.

These last few weeks I've walked through one of the most difficult seasons of parenting thus far. It's stretched me beyond belief, it's left me in tears more times than I can count, and it's shown me that hope is where I must set my gaze these days. Hope in what is to come and hope in what God says will be.

Believers have felt this way since the beginning of time. They've been stretched, chiseled, and sanctified. Faith has not felt easy and because of that - they had to hope in what God would do next. By the grace of God, the "next" thing God did over 2000 years ago was send His son.

Hope came down, pierced the darkness, eclipsed the pang of sin, and left it's mark on us forever.

"For unto you is born this day in the city of David a Savior, who is Christ the Lord. And this will be a sign for you: you will find a baby wrapped in swaddling cloths and lying in a manger."
Luke 2:11-12

The hope of Jesus is found in the places we least expect. In the story of Christ's coming it was the glowing of a star that led the wisemen to find that the Hope for all the world had come. As you look to Jesus, rest in His hope. Rest in His joy and then experience His perfect peace.

Prayer Prompt

Father, thank you for the gift of hope. Without the hope of Jesus I would have no joy and no peace. Help me walk forward faithfully when life feels strangely dim. Keep me steadfast and hungry for you. Let my heart be a light that glows your grace and mercy into this world. In Jesus' name, amen.

Takeaway

_____

_____

_____

_____

_____

_____

_____

_____

_____

_____

_____

_____

_____

May the God of hope fill you with all joy and peace in believing, so that by the power of the Holy Spirit you may abound in hope.

Romans 15:13

By His Cradle We Stand

And the angel said to them, "Fear not, for behold, I bring you good news of great joy that will be for all the people..." Luke 2:10

Standing up for the things we believe in shows what we value the most. For me, I will always stand up and stand firm for my faith, my family, and anything else God has called me to keep sacred. I do this because I love my Savior. He calls me to obedience and I understand the importance of keeping my covenant promise with Him. If Jesus stands in the gap for me, I must stand up for Him where God has me.

We see in the story of Jesus' birth that the Wise Men were called to follow the star, and they went to find the Savior of the world. Before they went on their journey, King Herod heard of the news about Jesus and panicked. He sent them there with a mission to report back to him that Jesus was indeed where God said He would be. God then used the Wise Men to protect our Savior. He gave them a dream and told them to warn Mary and Jospeh to flee.

"After listening to the king, they went on their way. And behold, the star that they had seen when it rose went before them until it came to rest over the place where the child was. When they saw the star, they rejoiced exceedingly with great joy...And being warned in a dream not to return to Herod, they departed to their own country by another way."
Luke 2:9-10,12

The Wise Men stood up and stood firm to protect the Savior of the world. They trusted the call God had given them and held fast to their commitment to Him. Their commitment shows us how we must live for Jesus, too. Ready and willing to stand up for Him - no matter what.

Stand up. Stand firm. Stand for Jesus.

Prayer Prompt

Father, what an example we have been given by the obedience of the Wise Men. Thank you for the way you led them and praise God for their obedience. Help me live like them. With a bold, willing, firm, and committed heart to you. In Jesus' name, amen.

Takeaway

_____

_____

_____

_____

_____

_____

_____

_____

_____

_____

_____

_____

And the angel said to them, "Fear not, for behold, I bring you good news of great joy that will be for all the people..."

Luke 2:10

A Star Sweetly Gleaming

The heavens declare the glory of God, and the sky above proclaims his handiwork. Psalm 19:1

I loved looking at the stars when I was little, it was an activity that made it feel as if life stood still. It was quiet, refreshing, and brought a spark of joy. I remember being keenly intentional as I'd find the perfect comfy spot to lay, settle in, look up, and be amazed.

However, when I was little, I never looked at the stars and thought much about the One who created them - it was only a beautiful sight to set my gaze on. Now having my own children, I want to be sure they know these stars are so much more than a beautiful thing to look at. I want them to know who created every single one, who hung them in their places, and that it is He who makes them shine so brightly. I want them to know what a gift of grace it is for God to give us yet another tangible reminder of how He sends light to pierce the darkness.

A favorite scripture of mine is Psalm 19:1, "the heavens declare the glory of God, and the sky above proclaims his handiwork." It's the works of His hands that light up our sky each night. Amazing, right? And it's the works of His hands that lit up the same sky just 2000 years earlier that shone so brightly that a star led men to find what God had promised. "And this will be a sign for you: you will find a baby wrapped in swaddling cloths and lying in a manger."
Luke 2:12

What God creates, His light will be revealed in it and through it. He has been faithful over and over again to prove that. Look for His light and proclaim the works of His hands.

Prayer Prompt

Father, thank you for sending your light to pierce the darkness. You've been so faithful to reveal your light through all creation. Help me seek your light and proclaim Christ to all I encounter. In Jesus' name, amen.

Takeaway

_____

_____

_____

_____

_____

_____

_____

_____

_____

_____

_____

_____

_____

The heavens declare the glory of God, and the sky above proclaims his handiwork.

Psalm 19:1

Here Come the Wise Men

And going into the house, they saw the child with Mary his mother, and they fell down and worshiped him. Then, opening their treasures, they offered him gifts, gold and frankincense and myrrh. Matthew 2:11

Who is someone that you'd love to share your most treasured items with? For me, I think of my children once they are grown. I imagine my son giving his future wife a piece of my jewelry. One picked by him with such intention and care. I picture my daughter walking down the aisle at her wedding with the beautiful dainty gold cross necklace my parents gave to me on my wedding day. These pieces are treasures, not just for what they are - but, for what they mean to me. I want to give my very best to the ones I love the most.

We see written in the book of Matthew during the birth story of Jesus that when the Wise Men went to meet the Savior of the world, they took their treasures. They didn't think to take scraps of a project, what was least expensive, or what seemed like a logical gift to bring a mother and her newborn. They took the very best they had to offer.

49

"And going into the house, they saw the child with Mary his mother, and they fell down and worshiped him. Then, opening their treasures, they offered him gifts, gold and frankincense and myrrh."
Matthew 2:11

This takes me back to what I shared at the beginning; I want to give my very best to the ones I love the most. Well, I love Jesus more than anything. So, what do I give to the One that I love the most, the One who died in my place, the One who made me right before God forever? I will give Him my heart fully. The best I can offer is to put Him in the place He deserves - King of my heart and Lord of my life.

Prayer Prompt

Father, I thank God for the gift of your unending pursuit of my heart. What grace it is to know that all you desire is for me to give you my heart fully and seek you in all areas of my life. Lead me to a deeper walk with you. In Jesus' name, amen.

Takeaway

_____

_____

_____

_____

_____

_____

_____

_____

_____

_____

_____

_____

_____

And going into the house, they saw the child with Mary his mother, and they fell down and worshiped him. Then, opening their treasures, they offered him gifts, gold and frankincense and myrrh.

Matthew 2:11

Lowly in a Manger

And she gave birth to her firstborn son and wrapped him in swaddling cloths and laid him in a manger, because there was no place for them in the inn. Luke 2:7

When you think of lowly what comes to mind? Often this word has a negative connotation connected to it, but God graciously redeemed it when He sent our Savior in the most lowly of ways. He used the birth of Jesus to show how humble beginnings can be the start of something extraordinary.

When Mary and Jospeh found their place at the inn, I wonder if Joseph felt a heaviness that he couldn't find any place better for his wife to give birth to their son. Not just any son, the Son of God. I wonder if he pleaded with God in his heart for a place seemingly more suitable. Or, was Jospeh content, humble in spirit, trusting what God had spoken to him.

It can be remarkably easy for us to downplay the moments in our lives that don't seem shiny and worthy. We wrestle and fight with the idea that for God to be glorified things must be extravagant and perfect.

God has revealed to us the way He desires our hearts to be postured and we can see it vividly in the way the birth of Jesus unfolded. He desires us to be eagerly expectant for the way He will show up in the lowly places we face as we journey with Him on this side of Heaven.

Luke 2:7 says, "And she gave birth to her firstborn son and wrapped him in swaddling cloths and laid him in a manger, because there was no place for them in the inn."

When the lowly place looks like there is no way for God to move in your life, remember where He made room for our Savior to be born. Not in a palace, not in a well-structured home, but in a manger.

Prayer Prompt

Father, thank you for working in the lowly. You've made it known to all the world that you work in the places we least expect. Help me look for you in the seasons of my life when I can't trace the working of your hands. In Jesus' name, amen.

Takeaway

_____

_____

_____

_____

_____

_____

_____

_____

_____

_____

_____

_____

_____

And she gave birth
to her firstborn son
and wrapped him
in swaddling
cloths and laid
him in a manger,
because there was
no place for them
in the inn.

Luke 2:7

In All Our Trials

Count it all joy, my brothers, when you meet trials of various kinds, for you know that the testing of your faith produces steadfastness. James 1:2-3

Life is a constant ebb and flow. If I'm being honest, I'm not sure which seasons feel longer. Sometimes the swells of the ebb feel as if I can't catch a breath. Then comes the flow and it feels like it's going so quickly I can't stop to take it all in. They can both be exhausting in their own way. Both can be marked by incredible trials, too.

We often believe that trials come in the absence of joy. I'm not sure why or how we've fabricated this in our minds, because it's just not true. The Word of God makes this eminently clear. He tells us in James 1:2-3, "Count it all joy, my brothers, when you meet trials of various kinds, for you know that the testing of your faith produces steadfastness."

God's Word doesn't say, "you will not face trials of any kind so long as your life is filled with joy." What it does tell us is that we will face trials throughout all of life, and to count it as joy that these trials will be a testing of our faith which will lead to steadfastness.

I think of the trials Jesus faced. They were constant. However, His hope and joy were constant, too. I know - He's the Savior of the world so of course He could be constantly hopeful and joyful. But let us not be so quick to write off our ability to emulate these attributes of Christ. We, too, can be joyful and hopeful in the midst of trials because Jesus was. We can seek to walk forward faithfully counting it joy when we face trials for the Kingdom.

Prayer Prompt

Father, you are faithful to see us through the trials of life. Help me to emulate your attributes no matter what circumstances I'm walking through. Keep me close as I journey with you. In Jesus' name, amen.

Takeaway

_____

_____

_____

_____

_____

_____

_____

_____

_____

_____

_____

_____

Count it all joy,
my brothers, when
you meet trials of
various kinds, for
you know that the
testing of your
faith produces
steadfastness.

James 1:2-3

Born to be our Friend

No longer do I call you servants, for the servant does not know what his master is doing; but I have called you friends, for all that I have heard from my Father I have made known to you. John 15:15

2024 marked many losses for me. The loss of friendship and loved ones. It was gut wrenching. It left me questioning why certain things happen and perhaps the hardest question of all, could I have done more?

I lost my very best friend at the beginning of the year. We shared everything together. Highest of highs and lowest of lows. As things began shifting in our friendship, it was as if God was trying to ease the pain of when the friendship would be no more. On a beautiful, oddly warm, February afternoon, the phone call happened. It would be the last time we'd speak. The tension was felt from miles away. Hearts were hurt and a friendship came to an end.

I've held tightly to John 15:15 as I've navigated this season, "No longer do I call you servants, for the servant does not know what his master is doing; but I have called you friends, for all that I have heard from my Father I have made known to you." Jesus came to be our Savior, and He also came to be our very best friend.

The pain in my heart has certainly been worth what I've gained with Jesus. He took what was so difficult and has made it into an area of my life that drew me in more deeply with Him. He showed me that while He sees me in my grief, He knows the weight of the loss. I can have a greater joy because of His love.

A friendship with Jesus breathes refreshment into our Spirit. It brings a security and hope knowing that the Savior of the world calls me His friend.

Prayer Prompt

Father, thank you for sending me the greatest friend, your Son, Jesus. He has mended my heart and filled a void only you could fill. Lead me to a deeper walk and faithful friendship with you. In Jesus' name, amen.

Takeaway

_____

_____

_____

_____

_____

_____

_____

_____

_____

_____

_____

_____

_____

No longer do I call you servants, for the servant does not know what his master is doing; but I have called you friends, for all that I have heard from my Father I have made known to you.

John 15:15

He Knows Our Need

"I have said these things to you, that in me you may have peace. In the world you will have tribulation. But take heart; I have overcome the world." John 16:33

What does your list of needs look like? Long or short, desperate or doable, heavy-laden or light? While this often changes depending on our season of life, I think we can all agree our lists feel a little longer and a little heavier than we'd like them to be.

This world is hard. There is sadness, destruction, and devastation all around us. At times it has me wondering if we will ever have an opportunity in this world to feel like we have a second to come up for air? When this question arises, the Holy Spirit always meets me with this, John 16:33, "I have said these things to you, that in me you may have peace. In the world you will have tribulation. But take heart; I have overcome the world."

Because of Jesus, we can come up for air. Nothing we see or experience takes the Lord by surprise, and He meets us in it. He has overcome all the hardships we face, the devastations our country encounters, and even meets the needs of our hearts when sadness falls over us like a blanket.

When God the Father sent His son, He did so with intention. Not only to save us, but to save and redeem the broken world we live in. Because of Christ's first coming, we have hope in all that is to come. When Christ returns, all that is wrong will be made right forever.

Every ache of our heart will be gone, the lists in our heads growing with the needs we pray for will disintegrate like salt meeting water. He will wipe away the tears and make all things new. Take heart, He has overcome the world.

Prayer Prompt

Father, thank you for the victory you've given me in Christ. I praise for you the Holy Spirit's reminders of what your Word says. Help me hand every need over to you. In Jesus' name, amen.

Takeaway

_____

_____

_____

_____

_____

_____

_____

_____

_____

_____

_____

_____

_____

"I have said these things to you, that in me you may have peace. In the world you will have tribulation. But take heart; I have overcome the world."

John 16:33

Behold Your King

After listening to the king, they went on their way. And behold, the star that they had seen when it rose went before them until it came to rest over the place where the child was." Matthew 2:9

Since having my two children, I can somewhat envision what the moment was like when Jesus took His first breath on earth. When a baby comes into this world it's as if time stands still. Their cry is bold but tenderly sweet. Their sounds, squirms, and snuggles are unlike anything else in this world. Heaven meets earth and when Jesus was born, heaven came to dwell on earth.

As heaven came down to dwell among us, there was a King who upon hearing the news of Jesus' birth feared that his reign would be cut short. So, he inquired of this "king of the Jews" and sent the wise men to gather all the details, and out of the hardness of his heart- he wanted Jesus to be erased forever.

Matthew 2:9 says, "After listening to the king, they went on their way. And behold, the star that they had seen when it rose went before them until it came to rest over the place where the child was." God used the light of the star to lead the wise men. As it rested over the place they would find Jesus, they rejoiced.

Behold, our King had come.
Prophecy was fulfilled.
Heaven was now dwelling among us.

What a King we serve. He came in the humblest of ways. Living and learning just as we have - though without sin. Growing from toddler, to child, to teen, and to young adult. Maturing in stature and knowledge as God paved the way for His ministry to unfold. Our King Jesus, who came as a baby, wrapped in swaddled cloths, is reigning and will reign as King for all eternity.

Prayer Prompt

Father, thank you for sending our King Jesus who would dwell among His people. Please give me the opportunity this season to share the story of Christ's coming and what a gift of grace is it to walk with Him. In Jesus' name, amen.

Takeaway

After listening to the king, they went on their way. And behold, the star that they had seen when it rose went before them until it came to rest over the place where the child was."

Matthew 2:9

His Law is Love

She came up behind him and touched the fringe of his garment, and immediately her discharge of blood ceased.
Luke 8:44

When you first experienced the love of God what did you feel? Overwhelmed, grateful, tear-filled, or hopeful? I think I felt all of those and then some. Experiencing and grasping the love of God changed my life forever. I quickly realized that though I was not worthy of God's love, He chose to love me anyway.

Once His love eclipsed my life it cut off shackles, removed fears, and freed me of sin habits I'd been tangled in for years. His love set me free, and as someone who grew up in the church yet kept Jesus at arm's length throughout my tweens, teens, and into my young adulthood years, this new freedom in Christ was remarkable.

Do you remember the woman with the blood disorder we read of in Luke 8? Well, in a lot of ways I felt like her, and though my issue wasn't a physical illness of the body, I had an internal illness of the heart. I spent years trying to heal the brokenness in my life with choices that only left me more empty and more broken.

Luke 8:43-44 tells us, "there was a woman who had had a discharge of blood for twelve years, and though she had spent all her living on physicians, she could not be healed by anyone. She came up behind him and touched the fringe of his garment, and immediately her discharge of blood ceased."

Only by touching the garment of Jesus was she healed. This miracle is almost incomprehensible. Yet, because of the love of God, these miracle moments are evident in my life, and I'm certain they have been in your life, too. Let us spend this season of Advent seeking the miracles we encounter because we walk with Jesus.

Prayer Prompt

Father, thank you for the love you extend to my heart. Though I'm not worthy, you chose to graft me in. Help me seek you in this season and look for the miracles you're working. In Jesus' name amen.

Takeaway

_____

_____

_____

_____

_____

_____

_____

_____

_____

_____

_____

_____

She came up behind him and touched the pringe of his garment, and immediately her discharge of blood ceased.

Luke 8:44

His Gospel is Peace

Peace I leave with you; my peace I give you. I do not give to you as the world gives. Do not let your hearts be troubled and do not be afraid. John 14:27

If you could feel one thing for the rest of your life on earth, what would it be? Mine would be, the peace of God, which surpasses all understanding. Imagining a life of only peace sounds like the grandest vacation. I almost hate admitting that, but it's true. Living on this side of eternity means I won't always feel peaceful, but I can be filled with the peace that comes from walking with Jesus.

What I mean by all of that is this, when Mary received the news that she and Jospeh would have to flee Bethlehem due to King Herod wanting to kill their child, I'm sure she didn't feel peace. I'm sure there were moments where fear was felt, and tears were shed. They were human. They had feelings. They, too, would need to surrender all those things repeatedly in return for God's peace.

God knows that receiving the call that a loved one has been diagnosed with cancer won't leave us feeling peaceful. He knows our hearts will be gripped with sadness and grief. God knows when a mother learns she's having a miscarriage, her heart won't be thankful. She'll be overcome with emotions and have a lifetime of reminders that brings waves of pain.

When God gave us the message of Philippians 4, it was to encourage us in the hard. Philippians 4:7 says, "And the peace of God, which surpasses all understanding, will guard your hearts and your minds in Christ Jesus." This is an invitation for you and I to lean into the peace we receive in Christ. Let us do just that today.

Prayer Prompt

Father, thank you for your peace. In the seasons of life where grief, struggle, and pain come, remind me of the invitation you've extended to us to experience your peace in the midst of it. In Jesus' name, amen.

Takeaway

_____

_____

_____

_____

_____

_____

_____

_____

_____

_____

_____

_____

_____

Peace I leave with you; my peace I give you. I do not give to you as the world gives. Do not let your hearts be troubled and do not be afraid.

John 14:27

Chains Shall He Break

"For freedom Christ has set us free; stand firm therefore, and do not submit again to a yoke of slavery."
Galatians 5:1

Years ago, while meeting with a Christian counselor, I made a chain with links symbolizing what felt like strongholds in my life. Along with the stronghold, she asked me to write a specific scripture that spoke truth against the lie the enemy had tripped me up with. As the Lord helped me overcome these areas, I was able to cut a link off the chain. It was a remarkable example of what happens when Christ sets us free. The weight of the world lessens, and the hope of freedom gives way.

When Paul wrote the words we see in Galatians 5:1, "For freedom Christ has set us free; stand firm therefore, and do not submit again to a yoke of slavery" he was reminding us that once we have been set free from sin and death through Christ, we never have to go back to the strongholds that were keeping us captive.

This is what God desires for all of those who walk with Jesus. He wants all the chains that hold us back to be broken. He wants us to experience the riches of His glorious grace and mercy. He sent His Son to bring forth redemption and restoration. When we walk in the freedom of Christ, we are walking faithfully in the gifts God gave us because of what took place on the cross.

As we walk through this season that brings a visible darkness to the earth earlier with each passing day, let it remind us that though the world seems to grow strangely dim, the Lord has invited us to experience a chain breaking light. That light is Jesus.

Prayer Prompt

Father, thank for sending your Son, Jesus, to break every chain that tries to hold me captive. I pray to experience the grace and mercy of God as I walk forward in the freedom you offer me. In Jesus' name, amen.

Takeaway

_____

_____

_____

_____

_____

_____

_____

_____

_____

_____

_____

_____

_____

"For freedom Christ has set us free; stand firm therefore, and do not submit again to a yoke of slavery."

Galatians 5:1

Sweet Hymn of Joy

Let the word of Christ dwell in you richly, teaching and admonishing one another in all wisdom, singing psalms and hymns and spiritual songs, with thankfulness in your hearts to God. Colossians 3:16

This year has taught me many things - a few of the most important are: true joy comes only from Christ, my hope cannot be based on circumstances, and we should be more intentional with the depth at which we know our Savior. Preparing for this Advent season has stirred up a new joy and hope in my heart. A joy and hope I could only know by walking through grief. The grief has deepened my desire for stillness with Jesus and called me into a new rhythm for my soul to resist the distractions the world offers.

You see, over 2000 years ago when our Savior was born, a new joy had dawned! The long-awaited Redeemer, the Son of God was here; the giver of real joy and peace had come. In this moment the darkness was pierced forever and moving forward whatever the enemy would try to drum up - would only be momentary affliction. Finally, the distractions and disruptions, burdens and heartbreaks, loneliness and tragedies would never get the final say because a hymn of joy now filled the earth.

"Let the word of Christ dwell in you richly, teaching and admonishing one another in all wisdom, singing psalms and hymns and spiritual songs, with thankfulness in your hearts to God." Colossians 3:16

This new hymn has become the anthem of our hearts. It's the song that sings of the good news that has changed our lives forever. It reveals how we've been marked by grace. Touched by God's incredible mercy. Made new on earth and will be made whole in heaven for all eternity because of Jesus.

Let us live joy-filled and joyful because of King Jesus.

Prayer Prompt

Father, thank you for the joy we have because of Jesus. I pray my life would be one that reveals the glorious grace you've extended to me. Put your song of praise in my mouth and let me live it boldly on display. In Jesus' name, amen.

Takeaway

_____

_____

_____

_____

_____

_____

_____

_____

_____

_____

_____

_____

_____

Let the word of Christ dwell in you richly, teaching and admonishing one another in all wisdom, singing psalms and hymns and spiritual songs, with thankfulness in your hearts to God.

Colossians 3:16

O' Praise His Name Forever

Praise the Lord! Oh give thanks to the Lord,
for he is good, for his steadfast love endures forever!
Psalm 106:1

Speaking to a group of women on the seasons of manna and seasons of abundance I shared that both are promised to come as we journey through our life on this side of heaven. Manna seasons come and leave us aching for Jesus to scoop us up and take us out of our present circumstances. Abundant seasons bring forth a heart filled with gratitude and a hope, that just maybe, it'll never end.

As I shared stories from my own life and the why behind the way God uses these seasons, I saw the faces of each woman shift across the room. They, too, realized God uses seasons of manna to grow in us a persevering faith. This is a faith that will praise God through any storm. It gives us the grit we need to march forward in obedience because we trust God will work all things together. When God blesses us with abundance, this time is used to encourage us and bolden our faith for Jesus. It gives us a sense of rest and shows us His faithfulness from a positive vantage point.

We specifically see in the Bible a time when the people of God, the Israelites, experienced abundance in one breath and then needed to be given their daily bread to make it through the wilderness. Their journeying to the promised land reminds me of Psalm 106:1, "Praise the Lord! Oh give thanks to the Lord, for he is good, for his steadfast love endures forever!" His love is enduring and when we experience it, we trust that we, too, can endure what we're walking through because of Christ.

May we be believers that endure well, persevere when life is hard, and rest in the faithfulness of God. O' Praise His name forever more!

Prayer Prompt

Father, thank you for giving us the encouragement we need to persevere in our faith and life. Help me live boldly and faithfully for you. In Jesus' name, amen.

Takeaway

_____

_____

_____

_____

_____

_____

_____

_____

_____

_____

_____

_____

_____

Praise the Lord!
Oh give thanks
to the Lord, for
he is good, for
his steadfast love
endures forever!

Psalm 106:1

A Thrill of Hope

For from his fullness we have all received, grace upon grace. John 1:16

The season of Advent is an invitation into respite. A respite not just for our heart, personally, but for an entire world that finds itself routinely weary. Weary by the weight of the world, abounding tasks, and looming uncertainties. This season invites us to pause a little longer with hopeful expectation. It reminds us that though the darkness is seen all around, the thrill of hope has come - and His name is, Jesus.

This season brings forth a swell of reasons to celebrate the coming of our Savior. Not only does it gather us around tables with those we love, adds a layer of warmth and joy to the places we go, it brings with it the reminder of all that is to come - unending hope. Because Jesus is the one who came and pierced the darkness for all eternity. He shattered the world's unattainable standards that keep us up at night. He has offered you and me a grace sweeter than honey.

"For from his fullness we have all received, grace upon grace." John 1:16

Jesus' life is completely and complexly intertwined in all we do. It often seems like a glorious mystery. We see this in the way His grace abounds in our weakness, reminding us He has the final say. We see it in His extension of mercy as we try to walk faithfully with Him. We experience it through His unending love which continues to be the beacon of light we follow.

Prayer Prompt

Father, thank you for the gift you offer us through your Son, Jesus. I will rejoice because of the hope that has been secured. Still my heart as I seek you. In Jesus' name, amen.

Takeaway

_____

_____

_____

_____

_____

_____

_____

_____

_____

_____

_____

_____

_____

_____

For from his fullness we have all received, grace upon grace.

John 1:16

Merry Christmas

"And the Word became flesh and dwelt among us, and we have seen His glory, glory as of the only Son from the Father, full of grace and truth." John 1:14

The reason for the season has arrived. Christ was born this day! My prayer for you and me is this; when the tree is taken down, the glowing lights are put away, and the nativity scene is boxed up; we won't let the awe and wonder of the Advent season dissipate. We'll let the thrill of hope be the anthem for all our days to come. I pray our hearts have been ushered into a season that stirs us to have hearts that daily seek and celebrate our always truthful, all-sustaining, everlasting Savior, Jesus.

As we end our time together, I hope you've been steadied in the hope we have because of Christ and most of all that you feel nudged to eagerly and obediently know Jesus more deeply. He is faithful to reveal Himself as we seek Him diligently.

Trust in the ways the Holy Spirit leads you. Walk forward in faith trusting where God has called you to go. Lean into the heart of the Father who desires to show His glory through your life. Let the light of Christ be evident to those around you and invite them to experience the riches of God's glorious grace.

We have the good news that brings great joy to share with all people. Let us take this message of hope with the endurance and perseverance our faith has produced in us. To God by the glory!

And the Word became flesh and dwelt among us, and we have seen His glory, glory as of the only Son from the Father, full of grace and truth. John 1:14

Prayer Prompt

Father, all praise to you for the birth of your Son! I rejoice today and will rejoice all the days of my life for the gift I have received because of Jesus! I pray my love for you and your Son is evident. In Jesus' name, amen.

Takeaway

_____

_____

_____

_____

_____

_____

_____

_____

_____

_____

_____

_____

_____

"And the Word became flesh and dwelt among us, and we have seen His glory, glory as of the only Son from the Father, full of grace and truth."

John 1:14

Looking for more...

For resources to deepen your walk with Jesus, visit ChelseyDeMatteis.com. There, you'll find her 52-week devotional, "More of Him, Less of Me: Living a Christ-centered Life in a Me-centered World," perfect for centering your life on Jesus throughout the year.

If you prefer "little reminders," check out Chelsey's scripture card sets, which include options with just scriptures, scriptures with prayer prompts, and devotion sets.

Whatever it is you're looking for, you're sure to find something to meet you where you are on your journey with Jesus!

Resources here!

Made in United States
Troutdale, OR
11/29/2024

25452041R00062